HOW TO USE A NETGEAR ROUTER

Mastering Your Home Network: A Comprehensive Guide

Fitzpatrick J. Thompkins

Copyright © 2024 by **Fitzpatrick J. Thompkins**

All rights reserved

No part of this publication may be reproduced, stored in a retrieval system, or transmitted, in any form or by any means, electronic, mechanical, photocopying, recording, or otherwise, without the prior written permission of the author.

The information in this ebook is true and complete to the best of our knowledge. All recommendation are made without guarantee on the part of author or publisher. The author and publisher disclaim any liability in connection with the use of this information.

Table of Contents

Table of Contents	2
Introduction	4
Overview of NETGEAR Routers	7
Benefits of Using a NETGEAR Router	9
Key Features and Technology	12
Chapter: 1 Getting Started	15
Unpacking Your NETGEAR Router	15
Understanding Your Router's Components	17
Initial Setup Requirements	20
Chapter: 2 Installation	23
Connecting to Power and Input Devices	23
Router Placement for Optimal Performance	26
Using the NETGEAR Installation Assistant	29
Chapter: 3 Configuration	32
Accessing the Router's Web Interface	32
Basic Configuration Settings	35
Setting Up Wireless Networks (SSID)	38
Advanced Settings (Guest Networks, Parental Controls)	41
Chapter: 4 Security Settings	44
Changing Default Login Information	44
Enabling WPA3 Encryption	47
Setting Up a Firewall and Access Controls	50

VPN Configuration and Usage	53
Chapter: 5 Connecting Devices	**56**
Pairing Smart Devices	56
Troubleshooting Connection Issues	60
Managing Connected Devices	63
Chapter: 6 Maintenance and Management	**66**
Updating Firmware	66
Performing Router Resets	69
Monitoring Traffic and Usage	72
Scheduling Automatic Reboots	75
Chapter: 7 Troubleshooting	**78**
Common Issues and Solutions	78
Resetting the Router to Factory Settings	81
When to Contact NETGEAR Support	84
Chapter: 8 Additional Features	**87**
Using NETGEAR Genie App	87
Optimizing Router Performance	90
Utilizing USB Ports for Storage and Printing	93
Conclusion	**96**

Introduction

In the quiet suburban neighborhood of Maple Grove, Emily, a freelance graphic designer, struggled with her old, unreliable internet connection. Dead zones were frequent guests in her home office, and the slow speeds often interfered with her ability to meet client deadlines. That all changed the day she decided to upgrade to a NETGEAR router, guided by the newly acquired book, How to Use a NETGEAR Router.

As she unpacked her NETGEAR router, the sleek, angular design promised a new era of connectivity. Emily flipped open her book to Chapter 3, "Installation," where clear, step-by-step instructions awaited. The book not only explained the basics but also detailed optimal router placement for enhanced signal strength, which she hadn't considered before. Within minutes, she had her new system humming smoothly, its LEDs a reassuring green.

Chapter 4, "Configuration," proved invaluable. Emily learned how to access the router's web interface—a gateway to customization. She set up her main network and a guest network, all the while marveling at the simplicity the book distilled from what had initially seemed like a complex web of options. Security settings in Chapter 5 were next, where she fortified her network with robust encryption and a strong password, a step her old setup sorely lacked.

The real test came when Emily decided to host a video conference with a potential client. The NETGEAR router, now fully optimized, handled the high-definition streaming like a breeze. Remembering the tips from Chapter 6 on connecting devices, she had seamlessly integrated her tablet, phone, and smart TV into the network, each operating without a hitch.

Days turned into weeks, and Emily found herself delving into later chapters of the book. Chapter 7, on maintenance, taught her how to update firmware and monitor network traffic, ensuring her router performed well. Chapter 9 introduced her to the NETGEAR Genie App, a tool that simplified network management further, allowing her to make adjustments directly from her smartphone.

One evening, as she sipped her coffee and browsed through the concluding chapter of her guide, Emily realized the true value of her purchase. The book had not just taught her to set up and use her router; it had equipped her with the knowledge to exploit its full potential, transforming her home into a fully connected, efficient space.

Her neighbor, Tom, noticed the change too. After hearing about her success, he borrowed Emily's book to set up his own NETGEAR router. Like Emily, he found the detailed troubleshooting section (Chapter 8) a lifesaver when he ran into a snag during setup.

The book, How to Use a NETGEAR Router, became more than just a manual; it was a gateway to reliability, efficiency, and peace of mind in Emily's professional life. It transformed her approach to work and home life, proving that sometimes, the key to unlocking potential is just one good read away. And as more neighbors came knocking, intrigued by her newfound digital prowess, Emily knew she had not just invested in a router, but in a little masterpiece that sat neatly on her bookshelf, always ready to assist.

Overview of NETGEAR Routers

NETGEAR routers are renowned for their reliability, extensive range, and advanced features, which cater to both general consumers and tech enthusiasts. The essence of using a NETGEAR router lies in its ability to provide consistent and high-speed internet access, essential for everything from everyday browsing to intensive gaming and streaming. The routers come equipped with dual-band or even tri-band technology, which allows multiple devices to connect simultaneously without loss of speed or quality. This feature is particularly beneficial in households or offices where multiple devices are in use at any given time.

In addition to speed and connectivity, NETGEAR routers are designed with user-friendly interfaces that make setup and management straightforward. Users can access these settings through a web browser or the NETGEAR Genie mobile app, an intuitive tool that simplifies tasks such as network monitoring, parental controls, and device management. The app also helps in identifying and repairing common network issues, which enhances the user experience by minimizing downtime.

Security is another cornerstone of NETGEAR's offerings, with most models featuring robust built-in safeguards like VPN support, guest network access, and advanced encryption standards to protect user data from unauthorized access. Regular firmware updates are provided to keep the security measures up-to-date against new threats, ensuring the network remains safe over time.

Moreover, NETGEAR routers often come with Quality of Service (QoS) settings, which prioritize internet traffic to ensure that more critical applications receive the bandwidth they require. This is particularly useful for live streaming and online gaming, where low latency is crucial. Additionally, some NETGEAR models include features such as MU-MIMO (Multi-User, Multiple-Input, Multiple-Output) technology, which significantly improves the network's capacity and efficiency by handling multiple data streams simultaneously.

The broad range of NETGEAR routers means there is a model to fit virtually any need and budget, from basic models suitable for small apartments to high-end routers capable of managing the demands of large homes or offices. This flexibility allows users to choose a router that not only fits their specific requirements but also offers scalability as their needs evolve.

Overall, understanding how to utilize a NETGEAR router effectively can dramatically improve one's internet experience, ensuring stable connections, robust security, and efficient management of network traffic. This makes them a top choice for anyone looking to enhance their digital lifestyle.

Benefits of Using a NETGEAR Router

NETGEAR routers are renowned for their robust performance and reliability, making them an excellent choice for both home and business users who need a stable and secure internet connection. One of the standout features of these routers is the broad range of models available, which cater to different needs and budgets, ensuring there's a suitable option for virtually any situation. This versatility means that whether users are streaming high-definition videos, engaging in online gaming, or managing a home automation system, there's a NETGEAR router built to optimize their online activities.

A significant advantage of using a NETGEAR router is its user-friendly interface. The setup process is streamlined, which allows even those with minimal technical expertise to get their network up and running quickly and without hassle. Additionally, for those who wish to customize their network settings, NETGEAR provides advanced options that can be adjusted through a simple web portal or the NETGEAR Genie app. This app not only simplifies ongoing management of the router but also enhances user experience by providing features like network monitoring, parental controls, and guest access management.

Security is another critical aspect where NETGEAR routers excel. They come equipped with robust built-in security features that include support for the latest wireless security protocols, advanced firewalls, and VPN capabilities. These features help protect sensitive data from cyber threats and block unauthorized access, giving users peace of mind about the safety of their internet connection.

Furthermore, NETGEAR routers are designed to provide consistent and extensive wireless coverage. They incorporate advanced technologies such as beamforming, which directs the Wi-Fi signal to where it is most needed, and Quality of Service (QoS), which prioritizes traffic to ensure that high-demand applications receive the bandwidth they require. This results in fewer dead zones, reduced buffering, and a more reliable connection across the entire home or office.

The commitment of NETGEAR to innovation is evident in its continual updates and firmware upgrades that enhance the functionality and security of their routers. These updates ensure that the router's software remains up to date with the latest technologies and security standards, thereby extending the lifespan of the device and protecting the investment of the user.

In conclusion, the benefits of using a NETGEAR router are manifold, encompassing easy setup, comprehensive security measures, and dependable performance across a variety of applications. Whether for personal use, family, or business, NETGEAR provides an effective solution for anyone looking to improve their internet experience while ensuring their digital world is secure and efficiently managed.

Key Features and Technology

When considering the installation and use of a NETGEAR router in a home or office setting, the advantages it offers are both vast and significant, ensuring a worthwhile investment in network technology. Renowned for their robust performance, NETGEAR routers facilitate remarkably fast internet speeds, which is a crucial benefit for users who stream high-definition videos, play online games, or engage in any other bandwidth-intensive activities. This capability ensures that the user experience is smooth and buffering delays are minimized.

NETGEAR routers are also designed with advanced features like dual-band technology which allows them to broadcast on both the 2.4GHz and 5GHz frequencies. This flexibility is particularly useful in crowded areas where interference from other devices might be an issue, as the 5GHz frequency is generally less congested compared to the 2.4GHz frequency. The inclusion of multiple bands allows users to connect their devices to different networks based on the device's bandwidth requirements, optimizing performance for activities such as gaming and streaming, which are typically better supported on the 5GHz band.

The security protocols incorporated in NETGEAR routers are top-notch, with support for the latest security standards like WPA3 encryption, which provides enhanced protection against external threats. This is especially important in an era where cybersecurity threats are becoming more frequent and sophisticated. The routers also offer robust parental controls and guest network access, enabling users to manage who can connect to their network and what type of content can be accessed, which is a crucial control tool for parents.

Ease of use and setup is another hallmark of NETGEAR routers, emphasized by user-friendly interfaces and mobile apps like the NETGEAR Nighthawk app. These tools help users to quickly install and manage their network settings from anywhere, making the process accessible even to those who might not be particularly tech-savvy. Firmware updates and performance checks can also be managed easily through these apps, ensuring that the router always runs with the latest updates and optimal settings.

Moreover, NETGEAR routers are known for their reliability and durability. They are built to handle a wide range of temperatures and operating conditions, which makes them suitable for various environments, from busy office settings to more relaxed home use. The reliability extends to the provision of consistent internet connectivity, which reduces downtime and ensures that users can enjoy uninterrupted access to the internet.

Finally, NETGEAR's customer support is an invaluable resource for users, providing assistance through various channels including phone, chat, and community forums. Whether it's a simple setup question or a complex technical issue, NETGEAR's support ensures that users can get the help they need to keep their network running smoothly.

By choosing a NETGEAR router, users gain access to a product that not only meets their immediate connectivity needs but also offers the tools and features to manage and secure their digital environment effectively. This makes NETGEAR routers a strategic choice for anyone looking to enhance their internet connectivity and protect their digital activities.

Chapter: 1 Getting Started

Unpacking Your NETGEAR Router

Unpacking your NETGEAR router marks the first step toward setting up a robust and efficient home or office network. The process begins by carefully opening the box in which your NETGEAR router has arrived. Inside, you will typically find several key items essential for installation and operation.

The primary component is the router itself, which is the central hub through which all of your network traffic will flow. It's designed to be user-friendly with clearly marked ports and often includes one or more antennas, depending on the model, which may need to be attached or adjusted for optimal signal strength.

Alongside the router, the box should contain a power adapter necessary to supply electricity to your device. It's important to use the adapter provided by NETGEAR to avoid any issues with power compatibility that could potentially harm the router.

You will also find an Ethernet cable, usually a standard CAT5e or CAT6 cable, which is used to connect the router to your modem or directly to a service provider's network interface. This cable is crucial for establishing your internet connection, allowing the router to broadcast Wi-Fi signals to your devices.

The package often includes a quick start guide or an installation manual. This manual is a valuable resource as it provides detailed instructions tailored specifically to your router model. It guides you through the setup process, from connecting cables to configuring settings for the first time. The guide might also include information on how to access customer support if you encounter any difficulties during setup.

Some models may come with a CD or DVD containing software utilities or additional digital documentation. While the use of CDs for software installation is becoming less common, they are included to assist those who may prefer installing network management tools directly onto their computers.

Upon unpacking your NETGEAR router, it's recommended to inspect all components to ensure there are no physical damages or missing items. If any issues are noted, it's advisable to contact NETGEAR customer service for assistance or replacement before proceeding with the setup.

By carefully unpacking and inspecting your new NETGEAR router, you are preparing to embark on the journey of setting up a network that promises enhanced connectivity and performance. This initial step ensures that all necessary tools and instructions are at hand for a successful installation, setting the stage for a seamless digital experience in your home or office.

Understanding Your Router's Components

Understanding the components of your NETGEAR router is crucial for optimal setup and maintenance, ensuring you get the most out of your device's capabilities. Each component plays a specific role in the functionality of your router, from establishing connections to securing your network. Here's an in-depth look at these essential parts:

Power Adapter – This converts AC electricity from your wall outlet to the DC power the router requires. Ensuring your power adapter is correctly connected and suitable for your router is vital for reliable performance.

Ethernet Ports – Typically, NETGEAR routers have several Ethernet ports. One of these is the WAN (Wide Area Network) port, distinguished by its different color. This port connects the router to the internet via a broadband modem. The other ports are LAN (Local Area Network) ports for connecting devices like computers, printers, and gaming consoles directly to the router for faster speeds compared to wireless connections.

USB Ports – Modern NETGEAR routers may include one or more USB ports. These can be used to connect external storage devices directly to the router, allowing for easy file sharing across the network. Some models also support printer connections via USB, enabling wireless printing from multiple devices.

Antennas – External antennas on NETGEAR routers help to broadcast and receive Wi-Fi signals. The number and design of antennas can vary, impacting the range and strength of the Wi-Fi signal throughout your home or office. Some models feature internal antennas, maintaining a more compact design while still providing robust signal strength.

Reset Button – This small, usually recessed button allows you to reset your router to factory settings. This can be useful if you experience problems that cannot be resolved through the router's web interface. Resetting is also a crucial step when securing a used router, as it removes any configurations from previous users.

LED Indicator Lights – Your NETGEAR router will have multiple LED lights on the front panel. These serve as indicators of power, internet connection, Wi-Fi activity, and connected devices. Understanding what each light signifies can help quickly diagnose connection issues. For instance, a blinking light typically indicates activity, while a solid light may signify a stable connection or that a device is properly connected.

Cooling Vents – Routers can generate heat during operation. Adequate ventilation is essential to prevent overheating, which could lead to reduced performance or hardware damage. These vents are usually located on the sides or back of the router.

Wi-Fi Button – Some routers include a button to turn the wireless function on or off without accessing the software dashboard. This can be particularly useful for quickly securing your network when Wi-Fi is not needed.

By familiarizing yourself with these components, you can better understand how your NETGEAR router functions and maintain it more effectively. Each part is designed to provide secure, reliable connectivity, and knowing how to manage these components can significantly enhance your network's performance and longevity.

Initial Setup Requirements

Embarking on the journey to set up a NETGEAR router involves a series of initial steps that are critical for ensuring a successful and efficient network installation. The initial setup of a NETGEAR router is designed to be straightforward, allowing users of all skill levels to get their network up and running with minimal hassle.

The first requirement is to gather the necessary equipment. This includes the NETGEAR router itself, an Ethernet cable, and the power adapter that comes with the router. It's also important to have access to the modem provided by your Internet Service Provider (ISP). If the modem also serves as a router, it may need to be set to bridge mode to work properly with your new NETGEAR router, which avoids conflicts between the two devices.

Before powering on the devices, it is essential to find an optimal location for the router. The placement can significantly affect the performance of the network. Ideally, the router should be placed in a central location, away from walls and obstructions, and elevated off the floor, such as on a bookshelf or desk. This position helps in broadcasting the signal evenly throughout the area, minimizing dead zones where connectivity is poor.

Once the location is set, the physical setup can begin. Connect the modem to the WAN (internet) port on the router using an

Ethernet cable. This port is typically differentiated from other ports by its color or labeling. Next, connect the power adapter to the router and plug it into a power outlet. At this point, it is advisable to ensure that the modem is also powered on.

After the hardware connections have been made, the next step is to power on the router. The initial boot-up might take a few minutes, during which the router's lights may flash. Once the lights indicate that the router has power and is connected to the internet, the software setup can commence.

The software configuration typically starts with connecting a computer or a smartphone to the network broadcasted by the NETGEAR router. This can be done either through a wireless connection using the default WiFi network name (SSID) and password provided on the router's label or through a wired connection by plugging an Ethernet cable directly from the router to the computer.

Accessing the router's web interface is the next critical step. This is usually done by entering a specific web address noted in the router's manual—commonly an IP address like 192.168.1.1—into a web browser. The first time you log in, you may be prompted to enter default login credentials, which are also typically found on the router or in the manual.

Upon logging in, the NETGEAR installation assistant typically takes over, guiding the user through the necessary steps to configure the internet connection. This setup wizard will help configure network settings tailored to the user's specific ISP requirements and personal preferences. It's during this setup that users can set their network name (SSID), configure their network password, and make other adjustments to their network settings.

Finally, it's recommended to register the router with NETGEAR to receive support and firmware updates. Firmware updates are crucial as they not only improve the functionality of the router but also address security vulnerabilities.

By following these initial setup requirements, users can ensure that their NETGEAR router is not only functional but optimized for performance, security, and reliability, laying a solid foundation for a robust home or office network.

Chapter: 2 Installation

Connecting to Power and Input Devices

Connecting your NETGEAR router to power and various input devices is a critical step in setting up a stable and efficient home or office network. This process involves several important stages, each designed to ensure that your router functions optimally and provides a reliable internet connection.

The first step in the installation process is to connect the NETGEAR router to a power source. It is essential to use the original power adapter that came with the router to avoid any potential issues related to voltage or current that could harm the device. Locate a power outlet that is not subject to frequent on/off switching, as power interruptions could reset the router unexpectedly, leading to connectivity issues. It is also wise to avoid using a power strip with multiple other devices to prevent power surges that could damage the router.

Once the router is powered, the next step involves connecting it to the modem. This connection is typically made using an Ethernet cable. You should locate the Ethernet port on your modem—it's often marked as 'Internet' or 'WAN.' Take one end of the Ethernet cable and plug it into this port. The other end of the cable should go into the 'Internet' port on your NETGEAR router. It's important to ensure these connections are secure because loose cables can cause intermittent connectivity issues.

For households or offices with a landline that uses VoIP services, connecting the router to a phone line might also be necessary. This is usually done using a different port on the router specifically designed for this purpose, labeled 'Phone' or 'Line.' In setups that require this type of connection, ensuring the phone line is active and properly set up with your service provider before connecting to the router is important.

If your NETGEAR router supports DSL connections, you might need to connect it directly to a phone line using a DSL filter. This filter is crucial as it separates the data and voice signals, preventing interference from disrupting internet service. The DSL line from the filter connects to the DSL port on your router, setting the stage for configuring the internet service with your provider's settings.

After establishing the power and data connections, it's advisable to check the initial status of the router by observing the LED lights on the device. Each light typically has a color code to indicate different statuses: power, internet connection, and data transmission. A steady or blinking green light usually indicates good functionality, while red or amber might suggest a problem that needs troubleshooting, often detailed in the router's manual or support website.

Finally, once all physical connections have been verified and the router shows no signs of power or connection issues, the next step is to configure the router's settings via a computer or mobile device. This configuration involves setting up network names, passwords, and possibly adjusting settings like DHCP and DNS, depending on the network requirements.

By carefully connecting your NETGEAR router to power and the appropriate input devices, you set a strong foundation for a robust home or office network. Proper installation not only provides a stable internet connection but also ensures that the network is secure and ready to handle all types of online activities.

Router Placement for Optimal Performance

Placing a router optimally within a home or office is crucial for maximizing the performance and reach of your Wi-Fi network. When installing a NETGEAR router, several factors must be considered to ensure that its placement contributes to the best possible signal distribution and network efficiency.

The central placement of the router generally yields the best results. This strategy allows the Wi-Fi signal to spread evenly across the area, reducing the number of dead spots where the signal might degrade. Ideally, the router should be positioned in a central location within the home or office, away from the outer walls or corners, to avoid limiting the signal's reach on one side.

The height at which the router is placed also significantly impacts its performance. Wi-Fi signals tend to spread outwards and downwards; thus, placing the router on a higher shelf or mounting it on a wall can help in dispersing the signal more broadly. Avoid placing the router on the floor as this significantly hinders signal propagation.

Physical obstructions can severely dampen Wi-Fi signals. Materials like concrete and metal are particularly problematic as they can block or deflect the signal. Even glass and wood can have a noticeable impact. To minimize this, ensure the router is away from large metal objects like file cabinets, reinforced concrete walls, and large appliances that can interfere with the signal. Similarly, it should be positioned away from water sources such as fish tanks, as water can absorb the Wi-Fi signal.

Interference from other electronic devices can also reduce Wi-Fi performance. Devices like microwave ovens, cordless phones, and baby monitors should be kept at a distance from the router since they can operate on frequencies that may overlap with your Wi-Fi, causing disruptions. Additionally, in areas crowded with many Wi-Fi networks—such as apartment complexes—finding a less congested channel can significantly improve performance. Modern NETGEAR routers are equipped with smart technology that can automatically select the least congested channel to optimize performance.

Visibility plays a role too. Although it might not always fit with home décor, having the router in a visible, open space, rather than tucked away in a cabinet or behind other objects, helps in reducing signal obstructions. The fewer barriers between your device and the router, the stronger and more reliable the signal will be.

Another point to consider is the directional reach of the router's antennas. Antennas can be adjusted to fine-tune coverage. In multi-floor homes, positioning antennas at different angles can help distribute the signal more evenly across different levels. Some

NETGEAR routers come with advanced beamforming technology, which focuses the Wi-Fi signal directly to connected devices rather than broadcasting in all directions. This feature enhances the efficiency of the signal distribution, improving coverage and speed, especially for devices that are further away from the router.

In sum, optimal router placement is not just about finding a convenient spot but involves strategic positioning to combat potential physical and electronic interferences. By carefully selecting the location, adjusting the settings, and considering the building's layout, users can significantly enhance their NETGEAR router's performance, ensuring a strong, stable, and speedy Wi-Fi network throughout their space.

Using the NETGEAR Installation Assistant

Using the NETGEAR Installation Assistant significantly streamlines the process of setting up a NETGEAR router, making it accessible for users regardless of their technical expertise. This tailored software tool is designed to guide users through the installation and initial configuration of their new router, ensuring that the device is properly connected and optimized for immediate use.

The process begins as soon as the router is connected to a power source and the internet modem. Users simply need to connect their computer or mobile device to the router's default WiFi network, which is typically printed on the router itself or included in the packaging. Once connected, launching a web browser should automatically redirect the user to the NETGEAR Installation Assistant interface. If it doesn't automatically redirect, users can enter a specific URL, often listed in the router's manual, to access the Installation Assistant directly.

The NETGEAR Installation Assistant first performs a series of checks to ensure that the router is correctly connected to the internet. This includes verifying the physical connections between the router, modem, and the power source. If any issues are detected during these checks, the assistant provides step-by-step troubleshooting tips to help resolve common connection problems, such as improperly connected cables or power issues.

Once the initial checks are complete, the Installation Assistant helps users configure their internet settings. It automatically detects the type of internet connection, whether it's DHCP, static IP, or PPPoE, minimizing the need for manual input and technical know-how. For users whose internet service requires a login, the assistant prompts for the necessary username and password. This ensures that the router can connect to the internet service provider and gain access to the internet.

Following the connection setup, the assistant guides users through the process of setting up their wireless network. This includes choosing a network name (SSID) and a strong password to secure the network. The importance of strong, unique passwords is often emphasized to help protect the network from unauthorized access. During this step, users can also configure separate guest networks if they wish to provide internet access to visitors without granting them access to the main network.

Advanced options are available for users who wish to customize their setup further, including parental controls, network speed tests, and firmware updates. The Installation Assistant often includes prompts or links to these settings, allowing users to access these features directly from the setup interface.

After the configuration is complete, the Installation Assistant typically performs a final series of tests to ensure that everything is functioning correctly. This includes checking that the router is online, that the wireless networks are active, and that connected devices can access the internet. Successful completion of these tests confirms that the router is ready for use.

To conclude the setup process, the Installation Assistant often provides a summary of the settings and changes made during the installation. Users are encouraged to save or print this summary for future reference, especially the new network settings and passwords. Some versions of the assistant may also offer to send this information to a user's email for secure storage.

The NETGEAR Installation Assistant is not just a tool for setting up a new router but a comprehensive guide that ensures users can quickly and effectively bring their home or office network online with minimal fuss and maximum security. This ease of use, combined with detailed guidance, makes the NETGEAR router a preferred choice for many looking to establish a reliable and secure network environment.

Chapter: 3 Configuration

Accessing the Router's Web Interface

Accessing the web interface of a NETGEAR router is a crucial step in configuring and managing the network settings to suit individual needs. This web-based interface, commonly referred to as the router dashboard, is where all the magic happens—from setting up wireless networks to enhancing security protocols. The process is user-friendly, designed to ensure that even those without a technical background can navigate it with ease.

To begin, ensure that the NETGEAR router is connected to the internet and that the computer or device you are using to access the router's web interface is connected to the router's network. This can be done either wirelessly or through a direct Ethernet connection. Once connected, the process to access the dashboard begins by opening any web browser on your device.

In the address bar of the browser, enter the router's default IP address which typically is "192.168.1.1" or "192.168.0.1". Alternatively, NETGEAR routers can often be accessed by typing "routerlogin.net" or "routerlogin.com" into the browser's address bar. These URLs serve as convenient shortcuts that route you directly to the router's login screen, bypassing the need to remember the IP address.

Upon entering the URL or IP address, a login prompt will appear requesting a username and password. For most NETGEAR routers, the default username is "admin" and the default password is "password". It's important to note that for security reasons, changing the default login credentials during the initial setup is highly recommended. If you have changed these details and forgotten them, you might need to reset the router to factory settings to regain access.

Once the correct credentials are entered, you will be granted access to the NETGEAR router's web interface. This interface is typically well-organized, with menus and submenus laid out in a logical structure. Users can navigate through various sections such as 'Wireless Settings', 'Network Map', 'Parental Controls', and 'Advanced Settings'. Each section is designed to control specific aspects of the router's operation, from basic network name (SSID) and password changes to more advanced functions like port forwarding and network security configurations.

Within the web interface, users can also monitor connected devices, check internet speeds, update router firmware, and back up current settings—an essential step before making significant changes to the configuration. The interface might also provide diagnostics tools to analyze network problems and monitor the health of the network.

For new users, the interface provides help sections and setup wizards that guide through the initial configuration and any adjustments needed. These wizards are particularly useful for tasks like setting up a guest network or securing the Wi-Fi connection with encryption, ensuring that all settings are optimized for security and performance without needing deep technical knowledge.

In conclusion, accessing and navigating the web interface of a NETGEAR router opens up a plethora of options for personalizing and securing your home or office network. By providing a user-friendly and comprehensive platform, NETGEAR ensures that users can maintain control over their internet connectivity, optimizing both performance and security to meet individual needs effectively.

Basic Configuration Settings

Configuring a NETGEAR router for the first time can seem daunting, but it's a straightforward process once you understand the basic configuration settings. These settings are essential for establishing a stable and secure home network. To begin, you will need to connect your NETGEAR router to your modem and power it on, ensuring that it is properly connected to your internet service provider.

Once the physical setup is complete, the next step involves accessing the router's web interface. This is typically done by entering the router's IP address in a web browser on a computer connected to the router. The default IP address for most NETGEAR routers is either 192.168.1.1 or 192.168.0.1. Upon accessing this interface, you will be prompted to enter a default username and password, which is often found in the router's manual or on the device itself.

After logging in, the first task is to change the default login information. This is a critical security step, as leaving the default settings can make your network vulnerable to unauthorized access. Choose a strong, unique password for the router's admin account to ensure your settings are secure.

The next step in the basic configuration is to set up your wireless network, or SSID (Service Set Identifier). This is the name that will appear on your devices when searching for Wi-Fi networks. You can set up different SSIDs for the 2.4 GHz and 5 GHz bands, allowing you to optimize the performance of your devices based on their compatibility and location relative to the router. It's recommended to choose a name that doesn't personally identify you or your location to enhance security.

Setting up the Wi-Fi password is another crucial step. Under the wireless security settings, select WPA3 if it's available, as it is the latest and most secure form of Wi-Fi encryption. If WPA3 is not an option, WPA2-PSK (AES) is a strong alternative. Avoid using WEP or WPA, as these are outdated and more vulnerable to security breaches.

For further customization and optimization of your network, you may also configure the router to operate on specific channels. Automatic settings are typically adequate, but in crowded Wi-Fi environments, manually selecting a channel can help reduce interference and improve performance. Tools such as Wi-Fi analyzers can assist in identifying the least congested channels.

Finally, ensure that your router's firmware is up to date. Manufacturers frequently release firmware updates to improve performance and security. Most NETGEAR routers offer an option in the admin interface to check and update the firmware automatically. Keeping the firmware up to date ensures that your router is protected against the latest threats and runs as efficiently as possible.

By carefully following these basic configuration steps, you can set up a secure and efficient network environment with your NETGEAR router, providing a solid foundation for all your home or small office networking needs.

Setting Up Wireless Networks (SSID)

Setting up wireless networks on a NETGEAR router involves a series of steps that enable both secure and efficient home or office connectivity. The process starts by accessing the router's web interface, which is typically done by entering the router's IP address in a web browser on a computer connected to the router. Once logged in, the user can begin the setup of one or multiple wireless networks (SSIDs).

The first step in configuring a wireless network is to navigate to the Wireless Settings page on the router's interface. Here, users can create a unique name for their network, known as the Service Set Identifier (SSID). The SSID is what will appear in the list of available networks on any wireless device. Choosing a unique SSID helps avoid confusion with neighboring networks and enhances security.

After naming the network, it's important to select the appropriate security options to protect the network from unauthorized access. NETGEAR routers support several security types, but it is recommended to choose WPA3, the latest and most secure protocol. If WPA3 is not available, WPA2-PSK (AES) is a good alternative. The security setting requires the user to create a strong password that will be needed by all devices attempting to connect to the network.

Advanced configurations can also be made on the Wireless Settings page. For instance, users can set up a separate guest network with its own SSID and password. This is particularly useful for those who frequently have visitors and prefer to keep their primary network private. The guest network option typically allows the owner to limit access to local network resources, such as file shares or printers.

In homes or offices where interference or signal overlap might be an issue, adjusting the wireless channel can enhance network performance. Most NETGEAR routers are equipped with automatic channel selection, which will choose the best channel based on the environment. However, users can manually select a channel if they notice connectivity issues. This is often necessary in densely populated areas where many networks might be operating on the same channel.

For users looking to optimize their network's performance, NETGEAR routers also offer the ability to operate on dual bands. This feature allows the router to broadcast the wireless network on both the 2.4GHz and 5GHz frequencies. The 2.4GHz band provides better coverage through walls and other structures, whereas the 5GHz band offers faster speeds at a shorter range. By setting up both bands, users can connect devices to the most appropriate band based on device compatibility and location relative to the router.

Once all settings have been configured, it's important to save the changes and restart the router to apply them. After the router reboots, wireless devices can be connected to the new SSID by selecting it from the device's Wi-Fi settings and entering the password created during the setup.

By following these steps, users can effectively set up and manage their wireless networks using a NETGEAR router, ensuring both secure and optimal connectivity tailored to their specific environment and needs. This process not only provides a robust connection but also gives users the flexibility to cater to diverse device requirements and usage scenarios.

Advanced Settings (Guest Networks, Parental Controls)

Configuring advanced settings on a NETGEAR router, particularly for guest networks and parental controls, provides a tailored and secure internet experience. These features are essential for managing who accesses the network and how they use it, aligning closely with the needs of modern users who prioritize both convenience and security.

Setting up a guest network is one of the standout features of NETGEAR routers. This function allows the creation of a separate network for visitors, ensuring that the main network remains secure and private. Guest networks are particularly useful in environments where frequent visitors need internet access, such as in homes that often host friends or in small businesses. The process involves accessing the router's web interface and navigating to the wireless settings where the user can easily activate the guest network. This network can be configured with a unique SSID (Service Set Identifier) and password, distinct from those of the main network. Customizable options such as limiting the bandwidth for guests, setting a maximum number of connections, or even scheduling availability times for the guest network further enhance its utility and security.

Parental controls are another critical component in managing the internet usage within a household or organization. NETGEAR routers come equipped with robust parental control features that help in filtering content, blocking malicious websites, and setting access schedules to restrict internet usage during certain times. This is particularly important for parents wishing to keep their children safe from inappropriate online content and to manage their screen time effectively. Activating parental controls involves accessing the router's dashboard, where specific websites can be blocked or allowed, and internet access can be paused for certain devices. Moreover, NETGEAR integrates with Circle with Disney, a popular parental control software that offers enhanced features like content filtering, usage insights, and even location tracking for mobile devices.

Both guest networks and parental controls can be managed remotely through the NETGEAR Nighthawk app, a convenient tool for users who might not always be at home but need to make adjustments to their router's settings. This app not only simplifies the initial setup process but also provides an intuitive interface for managing these advanced settings on the go.

Furthermore, these advanced configurations benefit from regular firmware updates provided by NETGEAR, which often include enhancements to security features and new functionalities for a better user experience. Keeping the router's firmware up to date is crucial in maintaining the effectiveness of guest networks and parental controls, ensuring that the router continues to protect and manage network access according to the latest standards and technologies.

In essence, the advanced settings for guest networks and parental controls in NETGEAR routers empower users to create a safe and customized online environment. Whether it's providing limited access to guests or protecting family members from harmful content, these settings offer critical tools that cater to the diverse needs of users, ensuring their internet experience is both flexible and secure.

Chapter: 4 Security Settings

Changing Default Login Information

Changing the default login information on a NETGEAR router is an essential first step in securing a home or office network. NETGEAR routers, like all routers, come with preset login credentials, which are usually a standard username and password that are the same across many units. This common knowledge presents a substantial security risk as it can be easily exploited by attackers to gain unauthorized access to the network. Therefore, altering these default credentials is a critical security measure that every user must undertake to protect their data and network integrity.

To begin changing the default login information, one must first access the router's web interface. This is typically done by entering the router's default IP address into a web browser on a connected device. The default IP address is usually something like 192.168.1.1 or 192.168.0.1, but this can vary based on the model. Upon entering the IP address, you will be prompted to enter the default login credentials, which can be found in the router's manual or on NETGEAR's official website.

Once access to the router's dashboard is gained, navigating to the 'Administration' or 'Advanced Settings' section is the next step.

Here, you will find options to change both the username and the password. When selecting a new password, it's crucial to choose something that is strong and secure. A strong password typically includes a mix of upper and lower case letters, numbers, and special characters. It should be unique and not easily guessed, such as simple sequences or common passwords.

After entering a new username and password, it is important to save the changes. Most routers will require a reboot to apply the new settings, during which time the network will be temporarily unavailable. After the router restarts, the new login credentials will be required to access the router's settings, so it's vital to keep them in a safe place or memorize them.

Beyond just changing the login information, users should also regularly update these credentials, especially if they suspect that the information has been compromised. Moreover, keeping the router's firmware updated is equally important as updates often include security patches that protect against new vulnerabilities.

By changing the default login information and taking these additional security measures, NETGEAR router users significantly enhance the security of their network. This simple yet effective step prevents unauthorized access, safeguarding personal information and enhancing the overall stability and integrity of the network. Remember, maintaining a secure network starts with securing the point of entry: the router's login credentials.

Enabling WPA3 Encryption

Enabling WPA3 encryption on a NETGEAR router represents a significant step in securing a wireless network, as WPA3 is the latest and most advanced Wi-Fi Protected Access protocol available. This protocol enhances the security of networks by providing cutting-edge cryptographic strength that is particularly important in guarding against external threats and ensuring the privacy of the digital communications within your home or office.

To enable WPA3 encryption on a NETGEAR router, you first need to access the router's admin panel. This is typically done by entering the router's IP address in a web browser on a device that's connected to your network. The default IP address is usually something like 192.168.1.1 or 192.168.0.1. Once you reach the login page, enter your admin username and password. It's advisable to change these from the factory defaults to something more secure as your first step in setting up the router.

After logging in, navigate to the wireless settings section of the interface. This section might be labeled differently depending on your router model but generally can be found under menus labeled something like "Wireless Settings," "Wireless Security," or "Wi-Fi Security." Here, you will find options to configure the security settings of your Wi-Fi networks.

Within the wireless security settings, you'll typically see a drop-down menu or a selection screen where you can choose the type of security protocol you wish to enable. To upgrade to WPA3, select 'WPA3-Personal' from the list of available security options. In some cases, the router might offer a choice like 'WPA2/WPA3-Personal' which enables a mixed mode that supports both WPA2 and WPA3 devices. This is particularly useful if you have older devices that do not support WPA3 but you still want to increase the security for devices that do.

Once you've selected WPA3, you will need to set a passphrase or network key. This key should be strong and unique, consisting of a mixture of letters, numbers, and symbols, and should ideally be at least 16 characters long. This passphrase will be required by any device that wishes to connect to the Wi-Fi network.

After setting the passphrase, save the changes to the router's configuration. The router may need to reboot to apply the new settings. Once rebooted, all devices previously connected to the network will need the new passphrase to reconnect under the new encryption standard.

It's important to note that enabling WPA3 encryption can sometimes lead to compatibility issues with older devices that only support previous forms of encryption like WPA or WPA2. If you encounter connectivity issues with older devices, enabling a mixed-mode (if available) or updating the device's wireless software might resolve the problem.

Beyond just enhancing network security, WPA3 also includes features like Forward Secrecy, which ensures that captured data cannot be decrypted even if the passphrase is compromised in the future, and stronger protection against offline dictionary attacks. This makes WPA3 an essential feature for anyone looking to secure their digital communications thoroughly.

In summary, enabling WPA3 encryption on a NETGEAR router involves accessing the router settings, navigating to the Wi-Fi security options, selecting WPA3 or its compatible mode, setting a strong passphrase, and updating connected devices. This process not only protects data but also enhances the overall integrity and security of your digital home or office environment.

Setting Up a Firewall and Access Controls

Setting up a firewall and access controls on a NETGEAR router involves several steps that together enhance the security of your network. The process ensures that unauthorized access is prevented and that your internet connection remains secure against potential intrusions.

Starting with the firewall, NETGEAR routers come equipped with a built-in firewall that serves as the first line of defense against cyber threats. This firewall examines incoming and outgoing data based on predetermined security rules and filters out unauthorized or potentially harmful traffic. To effectively set up your NETGEAR router's firewall, you first need to access the router's web interface, typically through a web browser using the router's IP address, commonly set as '192.168.1.1' or '192.168.0.1'. Once logged in using your credentials, which you should change from the default for security reasons, navigate to the security or firewall section.

In this section, you can enable various levels of firewall protection. NETGEAR typically provides options such as blocking proxy servers, ActiveX controls, and Java applets, all of which are common avenues for security breaches. Each of these settings helps to prevent potentially malicious scripts or software from entering your network unnoticed.

Furthermore, configuring access controls is crucial for managing which devices have permission to connect to your network and what type of content can be accessed. This is especially important in households or workplaces where children or sensitive information are present. Access controls can be set up through the router's web interface, under a section typically labeled as "Access Control" or "Parental Controls."

Here, you can create rules that specify which devices are allowed to access the internet, the times they are allowed to browse, and even the type of websites they can visit. These rules can be applied to all devices on the network or customized for individual devices, offering a tailored approach to network management. For example, you could restrict social media access during homework hours for a child's device or block certain adult content across all devices connected to the network.

In addition to website filters, NETGEAR routers often allow for setting up service blocking, which lets you control access to internet services by type, such as FTP, HTTP, or email. You can also configure schedules to automatically enforce these rules at specific times and days, providing automated control over when certain devices or services can be accessed.

Lastly, it's essential to regularly update the firmware of your NETGEAR router to ensure that the firewall and access controls benefit from the latest security enhancements and threat definitions. NETGEAR typically releases firmware updates to address security vulnerabilities, improve functionality, and add new features. These updates can be applied through the router's interface or the NETGEAR app, ensuring your network remains protected against the latest threats.

By diligently setting up and managing the firewall and access controls on your NETGEAR router, you effectively fortify your network's security, ensuring safer browsing and data integrity for all users connected to your network. This proactive approach to network management not only protects against immediate threats but also contributes to a more secure, manageable, and efficient digital environment.

VPN Configuration and Usage

Security settings are a cornerstone of managing a NETGEAR router, essential for protecting both the network and its connected devices from unauthorized access and various cyber threats. NETGEAR routers come equipped with a suite of advanced security features designed to provide robust protection. Users can configure these settings through an intuitive web interface or a mobile application, which simplifies the process of securing their network.

One of the primary security measures available on NETGEAR routers is the ability to change the default username and password. It's imperative for users to do this immediately upon setting up the router to prevent unauthorized access. Default credentials are widely known and can be a vulnerable entry point if not updated. The user-friendly interface of NETGEAR routers guides owners through this process, ensuring that even those with minimal technical knowledge can secure their device effectively.

Another vital feature is the support for the latest Wi-Fi Protected Access protocol, WPA3, which provides more robust encryption than its predecessors. This protocol secures the network by ensuring that the data transmitted over Wi-Fi is encrypted, significantly reducing the risk of interception by cyber attackers. By supporting WPA3, NETGEAR provides users with top-level security for their wireless traffic, which is particularly important in environments where sensitive information is frequently transmitted.

NETGEAR routers also offer advanced firewall protection, which monitors incoming and outgoing network traffic and blocks potential security threats. Firewalls are crucial for preventing attackers from exploiting vulnerabilities in the network to gain access or launch attacks. The firewall settings on a NETGEAR router are highly customizable, allowing users to specify exactly which types of connections should be allowed or blocked, based on their security needs.

For households or businesses that require additional layers of security, NETGEAR routers facilitate the setup of guest networks. These are separate from the main network, providing visitors with internet access without compromising the security of the primary network. This feature is particularly useful for preventing access to the network's main devices and sensitive data. It is easy to set up multiple guest networks with distinct passwords, and each can be configured with different access restrictions, further enhancing security.

Parental controls are another significant aspect of the security offerings from NETGEAR. These controls help manage and monitor internet usage, blocking access to inappropriate content and ensuring that children's online activities are safe and appropriate. The controls can be customized to filter content based on various parameters, such as age-appropriateness, time limits, and specific website categories.

Finally, the ability to regularly update the router's firmware is a key aspect of maintaining network security. NETGEAR routers typically offer automatic firmware updates, which ensure that the router's software is always up-to-date with the latest security patches and performance improvements. Keeping the firmware current is crucial in protecting against the latest threats and ensuring optimal functionality.

Through these comprehensive security settings, NETGEAR routers provide a secure, customizable, and user-friendly solution for both home and business environments. The emphasis on ease of use, coupled with strong protective features, ensures that users can enjoy a safe and stable network experience without needing extensive technical expertise.

Chapter: 5 Connecting Devices

Pairing Smart Devices

Pairing smart devices with a NETGEAR router is a fundamental aspect of creating a seamlessly connected and efficient smart home or office environment. This process, which links various smart devices such as smartphones, smart TVs, tablets, home assistants, and IoT (Internet of Things) gadgets to the router, ensures that all devices can communicate with each other and access the internet reliably.

The initial step in pairing devices involves accessing the NETGEAR router's network. Each router broadcasts its SSID (Service Set Identifier), which is the network name visible to devices searching for a Wi-Fi connection. Users must ensure that the SSID is not only visible but also distinct to avoid confusion with other nearby networks. Once the SSID is identified, the connection can be established using a secure password, set during the router's initial configuration to protect against unauthorized access.

For smart devices that support Wi-Fi, the pairing process is straightforward. In the device's Wi-Fi settings, users select the router's SSID, enter the password, and the device should connect immediately. If the device remains within the router's signal range, it will automatically reconnect in future without needing to repeat the setup process, unless the network settings or password are changed.

Advanced pairing options are also available for devices requiring a more secure or dedicated connection, such as smart home security systems. For these, NETGEAR routers support features like WPS (Wi-Fi Protected Setup), which simplifies the connection process. By pressing the WPS button on the router, and then activating the WPS function on the device, pairing can be achieved without entering a password, utilizing a secure handshake protocol.

In addition to traditional Wi-Fi connections, NETGEAR routers may include options for connecting devices through Ethernet cables. This is particularly useful for devices that require a stable and fast connection, such as gaming consoles and desktop computers. Connecting via Ethernet involves plugging one end of the cable into the router and the other into the device. This wired connection generally offers superior speed and reliability compared to wireless connections, reducing latency and providing a consistent bandwidth allocation.

Another aspect of pairing involves managing these connections through the router's administrative interface, accessible via a web browser or a mobile app like the NETGEAR Nighthawk app. Through this interface, users can see which devices are currently connected, monitor their bandwidth usage, and prioritize devices to ensure critical applications have sufficient bandwidth. This is particularly useful in environments where multiple devices are used simultaneously, as it helps to prevent any single device from monopolizing the network resources.

Furthermore, NETGEAR routers allow the creation of guest networks, an excellent feature for those who frequently have visitors and do not wish to share the main network's password. This separate network for guests can be set up with its own SSID and password, and it provides internet access while restricting access to the primary network's connected devices and stored data.

Finally, for homes and offices invested in home automation, NETGEAR routers support integration with voice-controlled assistants like Amazon Alexa or Google Assistant. This enables users to manage their network settings through voice commands, further enhancing the ease of managing connected devices.

Overall, pairing smart devices with a NETGEAR router involves a blend of straightforward Wi-Fi setups, advanced security options, and comprehensive management tools, all designed to create a reliable, secure, and user-friendly network environment. This connectivity not only enhances the functionality of individual devices but also integrates them into a cohesive and responsive system.

Troubleshooting Connection Issues

When using a NETGEAR router, troubleshooting connection issues is a key part of maintaining a reliable and efficient network. Connection problems can manifest in various forms, such as intermittent connectivity, slow speeds, or the inability to connect to the network at all. Understanding how to diagnose and resolve these issues can significantly enhance your experience.

Firstly, if devices are failing to connect to the network, it's essential to ensure that the router is powered on and all cables are securely connected. A simple initial step is to check the physical setup: ensure that the power LED is on and that the internet cable is plugged into the correct port. If everything appears correct, a power cycle of the router can resolve temporary glitches. This involves turning off the router, waiting a few seconds, and then turning it back on.

If connectivity issues persist, the next step is to verify the Wi-Fi settings. Make sure that the correct network name (SSID) and password are being used. It's not uncommon for devices to be configured to an old network name or password if these were changed during router setup or maintenance. Access the router's web interface to check these settings and update them on your device accordingly.

Another common issue is interference and range limitations. If the device is too far from the router or there are physical obstructions like walls and furniture, the signal strength may be too weak to establish a stable connection. Trying different locations for the router can improve signal distribution, especially in larger homes or offices. Additionally, devices that operate on the same frequency, such as cordless phones and microwave ovens, can cause interference. Switching the router to operate on a different frequency or channel can often alleviate this problem.

Sometimes, the issue may be related to the device's network settings. Ensuring the device is set to obtain an IP address automatically can resolve issues stemming from incorrect network configurations. To check this, go into the network settings of the device, locate the TCP/IP settings, and set the device to obtain both an IP address and DNS server address automatically.

For persistent slow speeds, it's important to check the number of devices connected to your network. Each device that is connected and active can consume bandwidth, potentially slowing down the network for others. NETGEAR routers often allow you to see which devices are connected and how much bandwidth each is using through their web interface. If specific devices are using a disproportionate amount of bandwidth, you might consider setting up Quality of Service (QoS) rules through the router settings, prioritizing critical devices or applications.

If none of the above steps resolve the issue, updating the router's firmware is another critical troubleshooting step. Manufacturers frequently release firmware updates to fix bugs, patch security vulnerabilities, and improve performance. Check the NETGEAR website for any available updates for your model and follow the instructions to apply the update.

Lastly, resetting the router to factory settings can be considered as a last resort. This will erase all the custom settings, so it is recommended to back up the router's configuration before performing a factory reset. Once the router is reset, you can reconfigure it from scratch, which often eliminates persistent or complicated issues.

Troubleshooting connection issues with a NETGEAR router involves a systematic approach to identifying and resolving common problems, ensuring that your network remains robust and dependable.

Managing Connected Devices

Managing connected devices with a NETGEAR router is an essential aspect of maintaining a secure and efficient home or office network. This involves not only the ability to connect devices such as smartphones, tablets, computers, smart TVs, and other IoT devices but also effectively monitoring and controlling their network access. The process is designed to be user-friendly, catering to both tech-savvy users and those with minimal technical knowledge.

The first step in managing connected devices with a NETGEAR router is to ensure all devices are properly connected to the network. This can be done using either a wired connection via Ethernet cables for devices like desktop computers and smart TVs, which provides stability and speed, or wirelessly for devices like smartphones and laptops. NETGEAR routers support the latest Wi-Fi standards, which offer fast speeds and reliable connections even when multiple devices are connected.

Once the devices are connected, the NETGEAR router's web interface or the NETGEAR Nighthawk app allows users to see a list of all connected devices. This list typically includes details such as the device name, IP address, and the type of connection it's using (wired or wireless). Users can rename devices to make them easier to identify, a helpful feature in networks with many connected devices.

The ability to monitor internet usage per device is another powerful feature. This is particularly useful in settings where bandwidth usage needs to be controlled to prevent any single device from monopolizing the internet connection, which can slow down speeds for everyone else. For example, if a particular device is streaming 4K video, it might consume a significant portion of the bandwidth, affecting the performance of other devices. With a NETGEAR router, users can view real-time bandwidth consumption and if necessary, set limits on how much bandwidth each device is allowed to use.

Access control is a critical component of managing connected devices. NETGEAR routers provide the capability to block unauthorized devices or limit access times during certain hours of the day. Parental controls can be set to restrict access to inappropriate content or to limit online time for children, enhancing safety and promoting healthier internet usage habits.

Furthermore, setting up a guest network is an effective way to manage who accesses the network. This feature allows visitors to connect to the internet without giving them access to the main network where personal files and other sensitive information are stored. This separation ensures the security of your primary network while still offering connectivity to guests.

Regular firmware updates are crucial for the security and performance of the router and connected devices. NETGEAR routers are equipped with the option to automatically check and install firmware updates, ensuring that the device is protected against the latest threats and is running optimally.

Overall, managing connected devices on a NETGEAR router involves an array of tools designed to optimize and secure a network. Whether through effective bandwidth management, robust security protocols, or user-friendly management software, NETGEAR provides users with a comprehensive set of capabilities to ensure their network remains both powerful and protected. This careful management helps maintain a balance between usability and security, making NETGEAR routers a suitable choice for both home and professional environments.

Chapter: 6 Maintenance and Management

Updating Firmware

Updating the firmware on a NETGEAR router is a critical component of maintaining and managing the device to ensure it continues to function efficiently and securely. Firmware is the software programmed into the router that dictates how it operates. Manufacturers like NETGEAR periodically release firmware updates to improve functionality, add new features, fix bugs, and patch security vulnerabilities that have been discovered since the last update.

To begin updating the firmware on a NETGEAR router, the first step is to log into the router's web interface, typically accessed via a web browser using the router's IP address, such as 192.168.1.1 or 192.168.0.1. After entering the required login credentials (which should be changed from the default for security reasons), the user will navigate to the 'Advanced' tab and then to the 'Administration' or 'Router Update' section depending on the model.

NETGEAR provides two main methods to update firmware: manually or automatically. For the manual update, the user needs to visit NETGEAR's official website and download the latest firmware version for their specific router model. It's crucial to ensure the firmware file matches the router model to avoid any compatibility issues. Once downloaded, the file can be uploaded through the router's update interface. During this process, it's important not to interrupt the power supply or close the browser window, as this can cause the router to become unresponsive or, in worst cases, permanently damaged.

The automatic update feature, if available on the router, allows the router to check for and install firmware updates by itself. This feature can typically be enabled through the same 'Router Update' section in the router's administration interface. Enabling automatic updates is recommended for users who may not regularly check for updates manually, as it ensures the router is always running the latest firmware with minimal user intervention.

After the firmware update is initiated, whether manually or automatically, the router will typically need to reboot. This reboot is necessary for changes to take effect and can result in a temporary loss of network connectivity. Users are advised to plan the update at a time when network usage is minimal to avoid disruption in internet service.

Beyond the actual update, it is good practice to periodically check the router's performance after the firmware update. Users should monitor the network for any unusual activity and verify that all previously configured settings are intact. Sometimes, updates might reset certain configurations, and users may need to reapply their custom settings.

In summary, regularly updating the firmware on a NETGEAR router is a straightforward but vital maintenance task that enhances the router's performance, security, and reliability. By following the appropriate steps for manual or automatic updates, users can ensure their network remains robust against threats and efficient in performance, thus extending the lifespan and efficacy of their NETGEAR router.

Performing Router Resets

Performing a reset on a NETGEAR router is a crucial maintenance step that can resolve numerous connectivity issues, such as slow internet speeds, frequent disconnections, or problems accessing the router's administrative interface. This process restores the router to its factory default settings, erasing all customized settings including the network name (SSID), password, and security settings. Understanding when and how to perform a router reset can greatly enhance the management of your network.

The first step in performing a reset is to identify the actual need for it. If troubleshooting steps like rebooting the router, checking cables, and verifying settings do not resolve the issues, a reset may be necessary. It's important for users to back up their current router settings before proceeding with a reset, as this allows them to restore their network configurations after the router has been reset to factory defaults.

There are typically two methods to reset a NETGEAR router: through the router's web interface or using the physical reset button on the device.

1. **Resetting via the Web Interface**:
   - Access the router's web interface by entering the router's IP address in a web browser. This address is usually something like

192.168.1.1 or 192.168.0.1. You will need to enter the administrator username and password.

  - Once logged in, navigate to the 'Advanced' tab, then look for an option that says "Revert to factory default settings" or similar. This option is generally found under the 'Administration' or 'Management' menu.

  - Click on this option and confirm that you want to proceed. The router will take a few minutes to reset and restart.

2. **Resetting Using the Physical Reset Button:**

  - Locate the reset button on the router. This is usually found on the back of the unit and may be labeled "Reset" or may simply be a small hole labeled "Restore Factory Settings."

  - Use a paperclip or similar object to press and hold the reset button. You typically need to hold it for about seven seconds, but this can vary by model. The router's lights will usually flash and then the router will restart.

  - Once the router has restarted, it will be in its factory default state.

After the router has been reset, it will need to be reconfigured. This involves setting up the network name (SSID), network password, and any specific settings such as parental controls, guest networks, or security protocols like WPA3 encryption. This is where having a backup of the previous settings becomes useful, as it can simplify the reconfiguration process.

It's also essential to secure the router after a reset. Default usernames and passwords are widely known and can be a security risk. Changing these to unique, strong credentials can help protect the network from unauthorized access.

Regularly updating the router's firmware is another important aspect of maintenance that can prevent the need for frequent resets. Manufacturers often release firmware updates to fix bugs, patch security vulnerabilities, and add new features. Keeping the router updated ensures that it operates efficiently and securely.

Understanding how to properly perform a router reset can help maintain optimal performance and security of your home or office network. It ensures that any persistent issues can be addressed effectively, restoring smooth and reliable operation.

Monitoring Traffic and Usage

Monitoring traffic and usage on a NETGEAR router is an essential aspect of maintaining a stable and efficient network. This capability allows users to keep tabs on how much bandwidth is being used and by which devices, helping to manage network load and to ensure that no single device hogs too much bandwidth, which can slow down the internet speed for everyone else.

NETGEAR routers come equipped with built-in tools designed specifically for monitoring traffic. These tools provide comprehensive insights into both real-time and historical data usage. By accessing the router's administrative interface, users can see detailed reports that include information such as the total amount of data transmitted and received, the breakdown of usage by device, and even what type of content is being consumed, such as streaming media or file downloads.

One of the most useful features for traffic monitoring in a NETGEAR router is the Traffic Meter. This feature allows users to set data caps, which can be particularly handy in scenarios where internet service providers impose data limits. The Traffic Meter will enable users to configure alerts so they can be notified when they are approaching their data cap, thereby avoiding potential extra charges from their ISP.

In addition to the Traffic Meter, NETGEAR routers often support Quality of Service (QoS) settings, which play a crucial role in traffic management. QoS allows the network administrator to prioritize traffic based on the type of service. For instance, high-priority traffic like VoIP calls and video conferencing can be prioritized over less critical traffic such as file downloads. This ensures that important tasks that require stable internet connectivity are less likely to be interrupted even when the network is under heavy load.

Advanced users can also benefit from more detailed traffic analytics available through third-party software that can be integrated with NETGEAR routers. These tools offer more granular data and sophisticated analysis, such as identifying which applications are using the most bandwidth or detecting unusual patterns that might suggest security concerns like malware activities.

Furthermore, for environments where multiple users or devices are constantly connected, such as in a small office or a home with numerous smart devices, monitoring network traffic becomes crucial. It helps in diagnosing network issues, like identifying a device that may be malfunctioning and sending out massive amounts of data. It also assists in enforcing network usage policies by allowing the administrator to see which users or devices are not complying with the rules set for network usage.

NETGEAR's commitment to providing robust firmware and software updates means that the routers continually receive enhancements in the area of traffic monitoring and management. These updates ensure that the routers can handle the latest internet protocols and security measures, keeping the network safe and efficient.

In summary, the ability to monitor traffic and usage on a NETGEAR router empowers users to manage their networks proactively. It helps in maintaining optimal performance, ensuring fair bandwidth distribution, and enhancing security, all of which are critical for both personal and professional environments.

Scheduling Automatic Reboots

Scheduling automatic reboots for a NETGEAR router is a vital maintenance strategy that enhances the device's performance and longevity. Over time, routers can experience memory leaks or slow down due to prolonged operation, and periodic reboots can refresh the system, ensuring it runs at optimal efficiency. Here's a closer look at the process and benefits of scheduling automatic reboots on a NETGEAR router.

First, the fundamental reason for setting up scheduled reboots is to clear the router's internal memory, which can become cluttered with outdated data that no longer serves a purpose but occupies valuable system resources. This is similar to rebooting a computer to improve its speed and responsiveness. For a NETGEAR router, a fresh start can resolve minor connectivity issues, improve network speed, and enhance overall device performance.

To schedule an automatic reboot, users typically access the router's administrative interface through a web browser. This is done by entering the router's IP address into the browser's address bar, which usually directs the user to a login page where they can enter their administrative credentials. Once logged in, the user can navigate to the system settings or maintenance section, where there are options for setting up reboot schedules.

In this section, users can specify the frequency of the reboots, which can be set to occur daily, weekly, or at any specific interval that suits the user's needs. Additionally, the time of the reboot can be chosen to minimize inconvenience. For instance, setting the reboot to occur during the early morning hours or late at night when internet use is minimal will likely go unnoticed by most users.

Another consideration is the potential impact on connected devices and ongoing activities. Scheduled reboots should be planned to avoid disrupting important tasks such as downloads, backups, or live streaming events. Some advanced router models can even detect idle times in network activity and perform reboots during these periods to further reduce any potential disruptions.

Moreover, automating the reboot process can help in maintaining the router's firmware and software updates. Often, after an update is downloaded, a reboot is necessary to complete the installation process. Regularly scheduled reboots ensure that any updates are fully integrated and that the router benefits from the latest security patches and performance enhancements.

Maintaining a NETGEAR router through scheduled reboots also extends to improving security. Reboots can disrupt potential unauthorized connections or activities that might compromise the network. This routine resetting of the system can act as a deterrent against certain types of network intrusions and exploits, particularly those that require a persistent connection to execute.

Overall, scheduling automatic reboots is a straightforward yet effective maintenance technique that keeps a NETGEAR router functioning reliably. It minimizes the hassle of manual reboots and ensures that the router's performance is maintained without regular user intervention. For anyone managing a home or small office network, taking advantage of this feature can greatly enhance their network stability and reliability, providing peace of mind that their connectivity infrastructure operates smoothly around the clock.

Chapter: 7 Troubleshooting

Common Issues and Solutions

Troubleshooting common issues with NETGEAR routers involves understanding the typical problems users might encounter and knowing the effective solutions to resolve them. These issues can range from connectivity problems, slow internet speeds, to more complex configuration errors. Here's a comprehensive look at some frequent troubles and their practical fixes:

Loss of Connectivity: A common problem with NETGEAR routers is the sudden loss of internet connection. This issue can often be resolved by performing a power cycle. Users should turn off their modem and router, wait for about one minute, and then turn them back on. This simple reset can help re-establish connections that have been lost due to minor glitches in the network.

Slow Internet Speeds: If users experience slower than expected internet speeds, checking the router's placement might be a good start. Routers should be placed in a central location, away from walls and obstructions and above floor level. This ensures optimal signal distribution. Additionally, users should check for electronic interference from devices like cordless phones or microwaves and adjust the placement of their router or these devices accordingly. Updating the firmware of the router can also enhance performance, as newer software versions often include optimizations.

Wi-Fi Connectivity Issues: When devices have trouble connecting to Wi-Fi, ensuring that the wireless settings are correct is crucial. This includes verifying the SSID (network name) and password. Users should also ensure that their device is not exclusively trying to connect to a different network band (2.4GHz or 5GHz) that may not be appropriately configured or supported. Enabling the router's guest network for testing can help determine if the issue is with the main network's settings.

Frequent Disconnections: Stability issues, where devices frequently disconnect from the router, might be due to outdated firmware or overloaded bandwidth. Users should check for firmware updates in the router's admin settings and consider allocating bandwidth through QoS (Quality of Service) settings to prioritize critical applications. If many devices are connected at once, disconnecting some or switching non-essential devices to a guest network can alleviate the load on the primary network.

Difficulty Accessing Router Settings: Users unable to access their router's web interface (typically accessed via a web browser at an IP address like 192.168.1.1) may need to check their computer's connection to the router. Ensuring the computer is connected either by Ethernet or Wi-Fi to the router, and not to a different network, is essential. If the default IP address has been changed and forgotten, a factory reset might be necessary, though this should be a last resort as it erases all settings.

Security Concerns: If users suspect that their network security has been compromised, changing the network's SSID and password is recommended. Enabling WPA3 encryption can provide an added layer of security. Regularly updating passwords and monitoring connected devices through the router's admin panel can also help maintain a secure network environment.

VPN Issues: For those using VPNs with their NETGEAR router and experiencing issues like slow speeds or connection drops, verifying VPN settings for accuracy is critical. Some routers also offer VPN client and server options, and ensuring these settings are configured correctly can resolve connection problems. If issues persist, consulting with the VPN provider for specific router settings or updates is advisable.

Addressing these common issues typically restores router functionality and enhances network performance. However, if problems persist after trying these solutions, contacting NETGEAR support for professional assistance might be necessary. Their expertise can help diagnose and resolve more complex issues that standard troubleshooting may not fix.

Resetting the Router to Factory Settings

Resetting a NETGEAR router to factory settings is a critical troubleshooting step that can resolve a variety of issues, including network connectivity problems, slow internet speeds, and forgotten passwords. This process restores the router to its original state with default settings, effectively clearing all custom configurations that may have been causing operational issues.

When a user decides to reset their NETGEAR router, it is essential to understand that all personalized settings such as Wi-Fi name (SSID), password, and security settings will be erased and reverted to their defaults. Therefore, it's prudent to record any specific settings or configurations before proceeding with a reset if they need to be reapplied later.

The process of resetting a NETGEAR router is straightforward but should be performed with caution to avoid unnecessary disruptions in service. Typically, there are two methods to reset the router: using the reset button on the device itself or through the router's web interface.

Using the Reset Button:
1. Locate the reset button on the router. This is usually found on the back of the device, often in a recessed section requiring a paperclip or similar tool to access.

2. Ensure the router is powered on.

3. Use the paperclip to press and hold the reset button. The required time to hold the button varies by model but is generally about seven seconds. Wait until the router lights begin flashing, indicating that the router is resetting.

4. Release the reset button and allow the router to reboot. This process can take a few minutes. Once rebooted, the router will be restored to its factory default settings.

Using the Web Interface:

1. Open a web browser and enter the router's IP address in the address bar. The default IP is typically 192.168.1.1 or 192.168.0.1.

2. Log in to the router's web interface with the current administrator username and password. If these credentials have been forgotten, the physical reset method will be necessary.

3. Once logged in, navigate to the Administration or System settings (the exact path can vary by model).

4. Look for a section labeled 'Backup Settings' or 'Revert to Factory Default' and follow the on-screen instructions to reset the router.

After the router has been reset, it will need to be set up again as if it were being installed for the first time. This includes reconfiguring internet settings, recreating your Wi-Fi network (SSID), and re-applying any previously noted custom settings such as port forwarding, parental controls, or security configurations.

It's also advisable to update the router's firmware to the latest version post-reset to ensure any known issues are resolved and the device is secured against vulnerabilities. Firmware updates can typically be performed through the router's web interface under the Administration or Firmware Update section.

Resetting the router is a powerful troubleshooting tool that can help overcome persistent network issues. However, it should be used judiciously since it involves setting up the router from scratch. By following these steps carefully, users can effectively reset their NETGEAR router and restore stable, secure network performance in their homes or offices.

When to Contact NETGEAR Support

Deciding when to contact NETGEAR support while troubleshooting your router can sometimes be a fine line between a simple DIY fix and needing professional assistance. Knowing the specific scenarios where expert help is warranted can save time and enhance your experience with your NETGEAR router.

Firstly, if you encounter persistent connectivity issues that resist basic troubleshooting steps such as restarting your router, checking cable connections, and ensuring that your ISP is not experiencing outages, it might be time to reach out to support. These issues could manifest as frequent disconnections, significantly slower internet speeds than your plan provides, or complete failure to connect to the internet.

Secondly, if you've followed the firmware update instructions detailed in your NETGEAR router manual and encounter problems during the process, contacting support is advisable. Firmware updates are crucial for performance and security, and issues during an update can lead to router malfunctions, including being unable to access the router's management interface or the router failing to boot up properly.

Security concerns provide another critical juncture at which to contact support. If you suspect that your network has been compromised—for example, noticing unauthorized devices connected to your network or unusual traffic in your network logs—NETGEAR's support team can assist in resecuring your network. They can guide you through changing passwords, updating security protocols, and checking for any vulnerabilities.

Performance issues that defy simple fixes, like adjusting the placement of your router or changing the channel settings to avoid interference, also merit a call to support. If your router does not distribute bandwidth efficiently, resulting in poor performance in certain areas of your home or office, NETGEAR support can provide advanced troubleshooting techniques and, if necessary, advise on hardware upgrades.

Additionally, if you experience problems with any specific features of your router, such as parental controls not working as expected, VPN issues, or trouble setting up guest networks, the support team can provide specialized guidance. These features can sometimes require complex configuration that may be covered in the router's manual, but practical issues in implementation or operational glitches often need direct support intervention.

Finally, hardware issues such as non-functioning ports, indicators that do not light up as expected, or physical damage to the router are clear cases for contacting NETGEAR support. In such situations, the support team can determine whether a repair or replacement is needed based on warranty coverage and the nature of the issue.

In essence, while many router setup and maintenance tasks are user-friendly and covered extensively in the NETGEAR router manual, there are circumstances where contacting support is not just recommended but necessary. In doing so, users ensure that they are maximizing the functionality and longevity of their NETGEAR products while maintaining a secure and efficient network environment.

Chapter: 8 Additional Features

Using NETGEAR Genie App

The NETGEAR Genie App is a central figure in maximizing the functionality and ease of managing a NETGEAR router, designed to simplify the process of networking. This app serves as an intuitive dashboard that provides users with the ability to access and control their home networks from the convenience of their smartphone or desktop, making network management accessible to both tech-savvy and novice users alike.

With the NETGEAR Genie App, users can quickly perform a variety of tasks that traditionally required logging into the router's web interface. One of the primary functions is the ability to monitor, connect, and control all devices connected to the network. Users can see at a glance which devices are currently connected, check the status of their Internet connection, and even block unwanted devices with just a few taps.

Another significant feature is the Network Map, which offers a visual overview of the home network. It allows users to easily identify each device connected to their network, view their status, and manage their connection settings. This can be particularly useful for parents wanting to monitor their children's internet usage or for identifying unauthorized connections.

Traffic monitoring is another critical feature provided by the NETGEAR Genie App. It enables users to review the amount of data being used by different devices. This can be crucial for managing bandwidth more effectively, especially in households where multiple devices are streaming video content or downloading large files simultaneously.

The app also simplifies the process of securing a wireless network. It guides users through setting up WiFi encryption, changing network SSIDs, and configuring guest access. This ensures that the network remains secure from unauthorized access and that guests can connect to the internet without compromising the main network's security.

For troubleshooting, the NETGEAR Genie App provides direct access to diagnostic tools that help identify and resolve common network issues. Users can run network tests, reboot the router, or update the router's firmware directly from the app. This level of control can significantly reduce downtime and the frustration associated with connectivity issues.

Additionally, the app includes a feature for setting up parental controls, which is invaluable for parents looking to manage their children's online time. These controls help in filtering content and setting time limits on internet usage, providing peace of mind for parents concerned about their children's online safety.

The NETGEAR Genie App also offers the convenience of remote access, which allows users to manage their home network from anywhere in the world. This feature is particularly useful for those who travel frequently but need to maintain control over their home network, whether it's to provide access to guests or to ensure that the network remains secure.

In conclusion, the NETGEAR Genie App is a powerful addition to the NETGEAR router ecosystem, providing an extensive range of features that enhance user experience and simplify network management. By integrating these capabilities into one user-friendly interface, the NETGEAR Genie App ensures that users can enjoy a stable, secure, and efficient home network with minimal effort. This app represents a critical tool in the modern digital home, helping users harness the full potential of their NETGEAR routers.

Optimizing Router Performance

Optimizing the performance of a NETGEAR router involves several strategic steps to ensure that the network delivers the best possible speed, coverage, and reliability. These steps encompass both hardware positioning and software configurations, tailored to meet the specific needs of the users' environment and usage habits.

To begin with, the physical placement of the router significantly influences its effectiveness. A NETGEAR router should be centrally located in the home or office to provide even coverage throughout the area. It's best to position the router in an elevated location, free from obstructions such as walls, large metal objects, and microwave ovens, which can interfere with the signal. Keeping the router away from windows can also prevent signal leakage, which enhances security by keeping the network more contained within the intended space.

The choice of the wireless channel can also impact router performance. Most NETGEAR routers automatically select the least congested channel upon setup, but manual adjustments might be necessary as local wireless conditions change. Using tools integrated into the NETGEAR interface, users can scan for and switch to less crowded channels, which is particularly useful in densely populated areas where many networks compete for the same channels.

Another critical aspect of optimizing a NETGEAR router's performance is ensuring the firmware is always up to date. Firmware updates not only provide new features and improvements but also fix security vulnerabilities and performance issues. NETGEAR routers can be set to automatically check for updates, or users can manually initiate the process through the router's admin page or the NETGEAR Nighthawk app, ensuring that the router operates with the latest advancements and protective measures.

Bandwidth management is essential, especially in environments where multiple devices are connected and competing for resources. NETGEAR routers offer Quality of Service (QoS) settings, which allow users to prioritize traffic based on the type of data or device. For example, a user can give higher priority to video streaming or gaming traffic over file downloads, ensuring smooth playback and responsiveness during critical use.

Furthermore, reducing interference from other devices is crucial. This can be achieved by adjusting the router's transmission power settings. Sometimes, reducing the power can minimize interference with other nearby networks and devices, especially in apartment buildings or close living quarters. Conversely, increasing power might be necessary in larger homes.

Regularly monitoring network performance can also provide insights into potential issues and help in maintaining optimal performance. NETGEAR's routers typically come with built-in analytics tools that can report on signal strength, device connectivity, and usage patterns. These tools can help users identify unauthorized devices, detect network intrusions, or simply understand their peak usage times, allowing for better network management.

Lastly, leveraging additional NETGEAR features such as Beamforming+ and MU-MIMO (Multi-User, Multiple Input, Multiple Output) technology can further enhance router performance. Beamforming+ improves signal strength and clarity by directing Wi-Fi signals directly toward connected devices rather than broadcasting in all directions. MU-MIMO allows the router to communicate with multiple devices simultaneously, which increases network efficiency and reduces wait time in multi-device environments.

By following these strategies, users of NETGEAR routers can significantly optimize their network performance, ensuring robust, efficient, and secure Wi-Fi connectivity tailored to their specific needs and environments. These steps not only enhance the user experience but also extend the useful life and functionality of the router.

Utilizing USB Ports for Storage and Printing

NETGEAR routers equipped with USB ports offer enhanced functionality, transforming a standard networking device into a versatile hub that can handle a variety of tasks, from shared storage to network printing. These capabilities provide significant advantages for both home and small office users, enabling easy sharing across multiple devices and centralized resource management.

One of the primary uses of the USB ports on a NETGEAR router is for network attached storage (NAS). By connecting an external hard drive or flash drive directly to the router, users can easily create a shared storage space accessible by all devices on the network. This setup is particularly beneficial for homes or offices where multiple users need to store and access large files like videos, photos, and business documents. The connected storage can also be used for backup purposes, providing a local, easily accessible backup solution for important data.

Setting up NAS on a NETGEAR router involves formatting the drive to a compatible file system, connecting it to the USB port, and configuring the router's settings through its web interface to enable file sharing. Users can create secure folders with varying access permissions, ensuring that sensitive information remains protected while still allowing for convenient access to less sensitive data.

Additionally, NETGEAR routers with USB ports can be configured for network printing. This allows a single printer to be shared among multiple users on the network without the need for connecting the printer to a computer. Instead, the printer is connected directly to the router's USB port. This configuration eliminates the need for a dedicated print server or for leaving a computer turned on to act as a print server, which can be both inconvenient and inefficient.

Setting up a printer on a NETGEAR router requires users to connect the printer to the USB port and then access the router's settings via its web interface or through a dedicated app like the NETGEAR Nighthawk app. From there, the router can be configured to recognize and manage the printer, enabling any device on the network to print documents directly to the printer without needing a direct connection.

The integration of USB ports on NETGEAR routers not only extends the functionality of the router but also enhances the overall productivity and efficiency of the network. Users benefit from centralized, easily accessible resources whether for storage or printing, simplifying the technology setup in a home or small office environment. These features, combined with the security and management options provided by NETGEAR's software, ensure that users can maintain a high level of control over their networked resources while enjoying the convenience of modern networked solutions.

Conclusion

In wrapping up a detailed guide on using a NETGEAR router, it becomes clear that NETGEAR's offerings in the realm of home and small business networking provide not just access to the internet but a broad suite of enhancements that elevate the typical networking experience. Users gain from a comprehensive toolset that boosts performance, security, and user management, catering to a broad spectrum of needs from basic browsing to complex data management.

Through the detailed steps outlined for setting up and configuring the router, one can appreciate the meticulous design and user-focused approach of NETGEAR. This makes tasks like updating firmware, setting up multiple networks, and securing the network accessible to users at all tech levels. The advanced features like dual-band technology and guest network capabilities allow users to optimize their network's performance and offer safe internet access to visitors without compromising their main network's security.

Security features are particularly notable, as they align with modern needs for robust protection against cyber threats. The ability to easily update security protocols and manage devices ensures that users can maintain a safe and efficient network environment. These are supplemented by quality of service adjustments, parental controls, and access schedules that contribute to a controlled and customized network usage.

The addition of USB ports expands the router's functionality, allowing it to act as a central hub for shared storage and network printing. This not only streamlines the workflow in a home or office setting but also maximizes the use of available resources, minimizing the need for additional devices and management overhead.

Moreover, the reliable customer support provided by NETGEAR, coupled with an active community and comprehensive resources, ensures that users can resolve issues and learn about their device's capabilities without undue hassle. The consistent firmware updates and intuitive management tools like the NETGEAR Genie app highlight an ongoing commitment to user satisfaction and device reliability.

Ultimately, investing time in learning how to use a NETGEAR router effectively is not just about getting online. It is about crafting a network that is robust, secure, and adaptable to the needs of its users, whether they are managing home automation devices, running a home office, or simply enjoying entertainment. This deeper understanding and practical application of NETGEAR's technology not only optimize the user's network experience but also amplify the overall value of their digital life.

www.ingramcontent.com/pod-product-compliance
Lightning Source LLC
Chambersburg PA
CBHW071102240526
45471CB00016B/2405